Mingkiri

A natural history of Uluṟu by the Muṯitjulu Community

Mingkiri *is an Aṉangu name for some small mice and marsupials. There are many other names for these animals, for example,* anula, wiltjinypa, murtja *and* tarkawaṟa*, but* mingkiri *is the name used mostly these days.*

Mingkiri

A natural history of Uluṟu by the Muṯitjulu Community

Edith Richards, Ruth Connelly, Wally Curtis, Trigger Derek, Kakaḻi Kinyin, Peter Kanaṟi, Billy Kayapipi, Kayu Kayu, Kata Kuṟa, Elsie Malpangka, Jimmy Muntjantji, Maureen Natjuna, Nyiṉku Jingo, Bernice Panata, Martha Protty, Puliya, Ruth Sitzler, Awulyaṟi Teamay, Malya Teamay, Norman Tjalkalyiri, Tony Tjamiwa, Barbara Tjikaṯu, Willie Wamantjangu, Tommy Wangi, Alan Wilson, Billy Wilson, Nipper Winmaṯi and Nancy Yungkama, all of the Muṯitjulu Community.

Compiled by Lynn Baker

IAD PRESS
Alice Springs

First published in 1996 by
IAD Press
PO Box 2531
Alice Springs NT 0871
ph: (08) 8951 1311
fax: (08) 8952 2527

Reprinted, 1998

National Library of Australia Cataloguing-in-Publication data:

Mingkiri: a natural history of Uluru by the Mutitjulu Community.
ISBN 0 949659 84 3
1. Desert fauna – Northern Territory – Uluru National Park. 2. Aborigines, Australian – Northern Territory – Ethnozoology. 3. Uluru National Park (NT). I. Baker, L. (Lynn). II. Richards, Edith. III. Mutitjulu Community (NT).
591.994291

Designed by Brenda Thornley
Photographs by M. Gillam (pages xi, 8, 9, 11, 12, 13(left), 14, 17, 20, 24, 25, 29, 34, 36, 41, 44(bottom), 45, 48), P. Canty (pages xiii, xiv, 3(top), 7(top), 10, 32, 32, 33, 33, 40), N. Gambold (pages 4, 13(above), 35), G. Fyfe (pages 6, 18, 23, 37, 44(top), 46), Parks and Wildlife Commission NT/R. Southgate (page 28), Parks and Wildlife Commission NT/T. Sandery (page 15), S. Breeden/Mutitjulu Community/Parks Australia (pages 3(centre), 5), SPA/Mutitjulu Community/Parks Australia (page 3(bottom)), J. Barry/ Mutitjulu Community/Parks Australia (page 7(bottom)) and Babs & Bert Wells/Nature focus (page 21).
Illustrations by Shawn Dobson (pages 19, 26, 27, 30, 34, 38 (raisin and fig), 42).
Map by Brenda Thornley
Cover design by Louise Wellington
Main cover photograph by Stanley Breeden/Mutitjulu Community/Parks Australia, additional cover photographs by Mike Gillam, Greg Fyfe and Peter Canty.
Films by Litho Platemakers, Adelaide
Printed by Griffin Press, Adelaide

Contents

Preface — vii
Acknowledgements — viii
Notes for the reader — ix
Map: Uluṟu–Kata Tjuṯa National Park and surrounding area — x
Introduction — xi

Chapter 1: Seasons and cycles — **1**
Ailuru – Drought — 4

Chapter 2: *Tjanpi, tali munu pila* – Spinifex, sandhills and sandplains — **9**
Itjaritjari (marsupial mole) — 13
Tarkawaṟa (spinifex hopping-mouse) — 14
Murtja (mulgara) — 15
Kuniya (woma python) — 17
Tjakuṟa (great desert skink) — 18
Kaḻaya (emu) — 19
Paṯiny-paṯinypa (Burton's snake-lizard) — 20
Mitika (burrowing bettong) — 21
Mala (rufous hare-wallaby) — 23

Chapter 3: *Wanaṟi* – Mulga country — **25**
Tjaḻa (honey ant) — 26
Ninu (bilby) — 28
Maḻu (red plains kangaroo) — 28

Wayuṯa (brushtail possum) _____ 30
Mingkiri (small mice and marsupials) _____ 32
Ngapaḻa (dwarf bearded dragon) _____ 34
Piṟurpa (tree-living gecko) _____ 35

Chapter 4: *Puḻi* – Rocky areas _____ 37
Aruṯju (fat-tailed antechinus) _____ 40
Kanyaḻa (euro, hill kangaroo) _____ 41
Tjilkamaṯa (echidna) _____ 42
Putukaḻya (dragon lizard) _____ 44
Tjuṉtaḻpi (long-nosed dragon) _____ 44
Araḻapaḻpaḻpa (crested pigeon) _____ 45
Ikarka (western bowerbird) _____ 46
Puṉtaṟu (little button-quail) _____ 47

Chapter 5: *Manta aṯunymankupai* – Looking after country _____ 49
Nyaṟuni – Burning off _____ 49
Tjunguringkula waakaripai – Working together _____ 51

Pitjantjatjara and Yankunytjatjara wordlist _____ 53
Pronunciation guide to Pitjantjatjara and Yankunytjatjara _____ 59
Bibliography _____ 64

Preface

Material used in this book was collected as part of a vertebrate fauna survey conducted between 1987 and 1990 in Uluṟu–Kata Tjuṯa National Park in the Northern Territory. Members of the Muṯitjulu Community, scientists from the Commonwealth Scientific and Industrial Research Organisation (CSIRO) and park staff collaborated in the survey to combine Aboriginal and scientific knowledge of the fauna found within the park. This information has since been used to assist in the development of management strategies for the park.

I compiled the information for this book from that provided by Aboriginal people during the survey. At the time I was the scientific project officer for Uluṟu–Kata Tjuṯa National Park and responsible for ensuring that research undertaken there maintained a high level of involvement of members of the Muṯitjulu Community.

During my four years at Uluṟu I was privileged to work in close collaboration with many people from Muṯitjulu who taught me a great deal about the country and its care. All of the information in this book came from Muṯitjulu Community members and was provided principally in language, usually Pitjantjatjara and Yankunytjatjara. Most of the translations were carried out by Susan Woenne-Green, the community liaison officer at the time.

I hope you find the information contained in this book as fascinating as I do and that it offers you some insight into the wonderful complexity of the arid landscape and the knowledge of this landscape held by its Aboriginal traditional owners.

Lynn Baker

Acknowledgements

Many people assisted in the preparation of this book, some directly and others indirectly, through the part they played in the Uluṟu fauna survey. I wish to thank them all for their support and co-operation. I would especially like to thank the many members of the Muṯitjulu Community who were involved in the survey, in particular, Edith Richards who provided much of the information, assisted in field survey work and participated in all stages of the project. Particular thanks also to Susan Woenne-Green, former community liaison officer for the Muṯitjulu Community, who facilitated the collection of much of the material used in the survey, as well as translated it.

I also wish to thank the members of the Uluṟu fauna survey team: Julian Reid, Anne Kerle, Stephen Morton and Kevin Jones of CSIRO, the Uluṟu–Kata Tjuṯa National Park ranger staff, Jeff Foulkes, and Linda Rive, who provided interpretive services; Uluṟu–Kata Tjuṯa National Park personnel, including Terry Piper, Bruce Lawson and Chip Morgan and particularly Jon Willis, the community liaison officer; Bradley Nesbitt, Helen McCann, Mark MacLean, and Sue Rammage and Warren Rammage for their editing assistance and suggestions in the survey report; and Angela Brennan, who edited the text of this book.

I also thank the Director of the Australian Nature Conservation Agency (now Parks Australia) for access to material from the non-Aboriginal sections of the survey report.

Lynn Baker

Notes for the reader

1. Names

Pitjantjatjara or Yankunytjatjara names have been used as much as possible in the text. Wordlists at the back of the book include other locally used names plus their scientific and English equivalents. A separate pronunciation guide is provided, and covers all Pitjantjatjara and Yankunytjatjara words mentioned.

2. Tjukurpa

In English Tjukurpa translates most commonly into Aṉangu (Aboriginal people's) Law. All life was created in the Tjukurpa by the ancestral beings (plant and animal) and the essence of creation continues to exist within each feature. Knowledge about plants and animals is therefore derived directly from the Tjukurpa, and is treated with respect: some of it lies within the realm of heavily restricted religious knowledge.

3. Aṉangu classification

Aṉangu and Piṟanpa (non-Aboriginal people) have different systems of taxonomy. Aṉangu classification of plants and animals is based in the Tjukurpa. Due to secrecy restrictions, much of it cannot be made public, and the following kinds of anomaly (as far as Piṟanpa classification goes) will remain a mystery. For example, while all goanna species have their own specific name, only some skink species do and the rest are grouped under a common name; *mingkiri* covers many species of mice and small marsupials, while some species of mice are classified in the same family as the kangaroo.

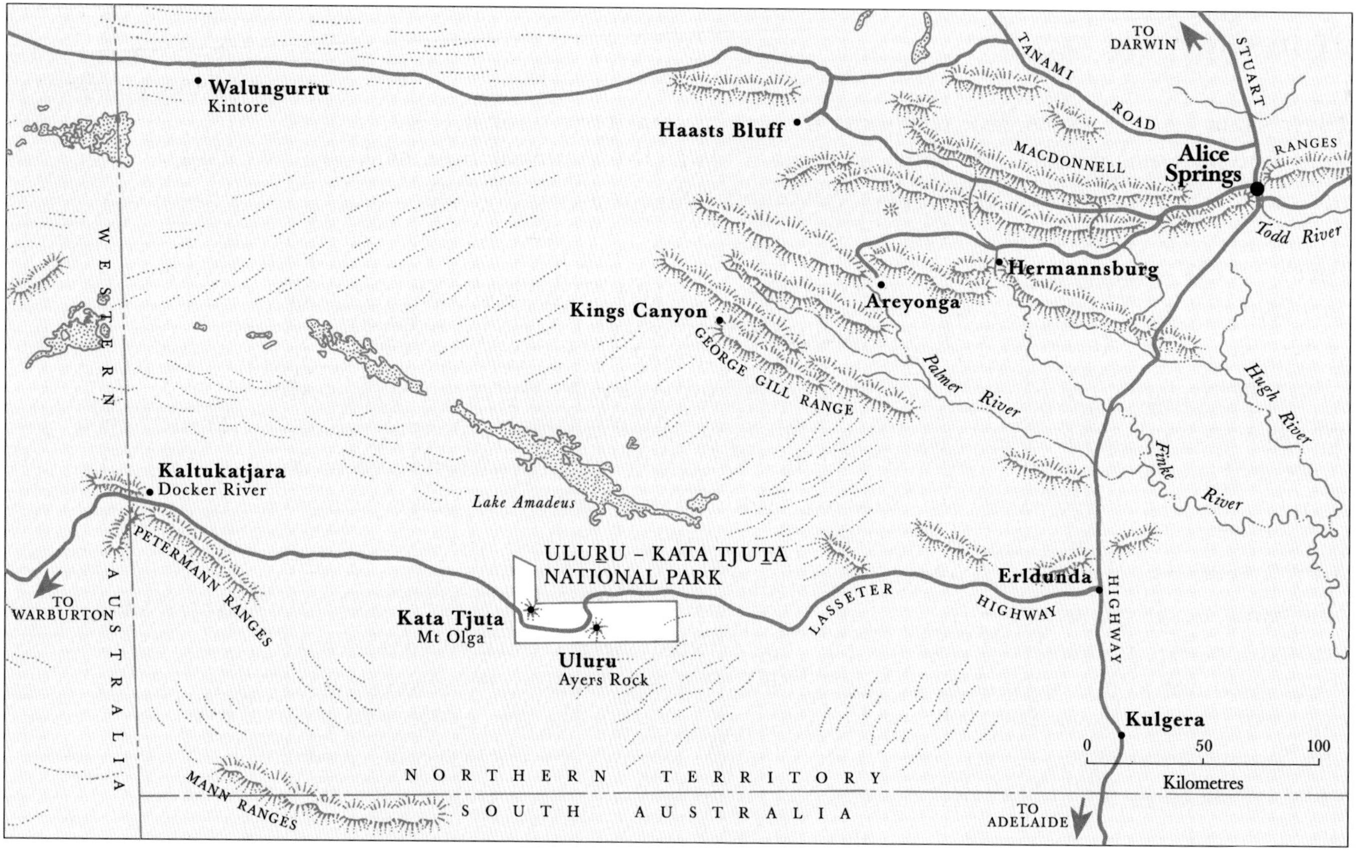

Uluru–Kata Tjuta National Park and surrounding area

Introduction

Uluṟu–Kata Tjuṯa National Park is Pitjantjatjara and Yankunytjatjara country. A long time ago white people took this land, Uluṟu and Kata Tjuṯa and all around it, from its Aṉangu owners. (Aṉangu means Aboriginal people; non-Aboriginal people are called Piṟanpa.)

Aṉangu won back this land in 1985, and they leased it to the Australian National Parks and Wildlife Service (now Parks Australia) to run as a national park. Before 1985, Europeans called it Ayers Rock and the Olgas. Now it is back to its original names: Uluṟu and Kata Tjuṯa. The park is looked after by both Aṉangu and Piṟanpa rangers, but Aṉangu manage it. The majority of members on the Board of Management, including the chair, are Aṉangu.

Aṉangu always welcome Piṟanpa to this special place. Yankunytjatjara people say, *"Pukuḻ ngalyayanama Aṉanguku ngurakutu."* Pitjantjatjara people say, *"Pukuḻpa pitjama Aṉanguku ngurakutu."* They are both saying, "Welcome to our Aboriginal land."

Uluṟu: an important place of Aṉangu Law.

Yankunytjatjara
pronounced:
young goon jarrer

Pitjantjatjara
pigeon jarrer

Aṉangu
ah nung oo

Piṟanpa
peer un pah

Uluṟu
ool oo roo

Kata Tjuṯa
kah dah **jaw** dah

Anangu
(Aboriginal people)
ah nung oo

Uluṟu   *(Ayers Rock)*
ool oo roo

Kata Tjuṯa
(Mt Olga)
kah dah **jaw** dah

Tjukurpa
jook oor pah

mingkiri
ming gear ree

When visitors come to Uluṟu–Kata Tjuṯa National Park they are fascinated by the country: the strong colours, the different plants and the way the landscape changes from rocky country to wide open sandplains.

A few years ago, from 1987 to 1990, Anangu worked with CSIRO scientists and national park staff surveying the animals and plants and setting up a proper way to manage the park. Some of that information has been written down in this book, so that visitors have a better understanding of this place – Anangu way. It describes how Anangu recognise the seasons and the importance of drought and fire on the animals of the park. It also describes how the landscape changes, from around Uluṟu and Kata Tjuṯa to the sand dunes and mulga country, and it talks about some of the different types of plants and animals that live in these places.

Visitors often think there are very few animals living here. That is because most of the animals only come out at night; the best way to find them is by looking for their tracks in the sand. Many of the reptiles are around during the day but move quickly from cover to cover making it hard to see them.

There are many ways Anangu get to know about the animals and how they live. By far the most important way of learning these things is through the Tjukurpa, or the Anangu Law. Some white people also call this the Dreaming. The Tjukurpa tells how the landscape, animals, plants and people were made and what they mean for one another. The Tjukurpa is in everything. It is in the rocks, in the trees, even in the mice, *mingkiri*. It contains the rules for how Anangu must live. It tells them about their spirit lives and how they should act together, in a family. It shows Anangu how to look after country. Anangu have to look after all these things. It is their religion.

Aṉangu
ah nung oo

Piṟanpa
peer un pah

Tjukurpa
jook oor pah

Aṉangu learn about the Tjukurpa from their parents and grandparents. They start learning when they are little kids and never stop until they are old people. They are taught how to recognise the tracks and burrows of animals, how the clouds move about and other things about the weather. From olden times they have had to rely on this knowledge to survive. They depend on it for food, shelter and tools. These days it is a bit different. People can get things from the store, or by driving into town. But it is still important to know all this, because it is spiritual knowledge. So Aṉangu do not forget the Tjukurpa; they still know how to find bushtucker and look after their country.

There are things, however, which Aṉangu cannot talk about too much. A lot of what comes from the Tjukurpa is sacred – restricted information. What is in this book is okay; it is public information. But it is not possible to talk about those other things, even though some people might want to know, or it might be important to scientists. It is important for the children and Piṟanpa to respect this because if the Tjukurpa goes, it is gone. It is gone for good, and then no-one will know how to care for country the Aṉangu way.

Kata-Tjuṯa glimpsed through desert oaks at sunrise.

Chapter 1

Seasons and cycles

Hot, dry and freezing cold – that is how it is in this country. Sometimes there is plenty of food around, the animals are fat and there is plenty to eat. Sometimes it is cold. The snakes and lizards sleep and the kangaroos are skinny. Sometimes it is too dry and the animals and plants finish up. They die. It is like that here.

The seasons here are different to other places. Different but the same. Like everywhere, there is a hot time and a cold time and good growing times in between. But they are not called summer, winter, autumn and spring.

They are named after the way the weather is. For example, the warm north-west winds around August and September give this time the name *piriya-piriya.* This is a good growing time like spring, and good for hunting kangaroos, but it is followed by a time when plant food is scarce, called *mai wiyaringkupai*, or *kuli*, when it is hot, dry and stormy. Big clouds called *marutjara* pile up in the sky and there is a lot of thunder and lightning, but not much rain, if any. There is not much food around at this time, and lightning strikes can start fires.

Then *utuwari* clouds arrive around January. These clouds come up from the south at the same time as the wind comes from the west. They can bring rain, but rain does not always come. It is still very warm, but it can be a good growing time. If the rains are good there is plenty of fruit and seeds and the animals get fat. Anangu call this time *itjanu*, which means lush green growth. It is also called *inuntji*, after the yellow, fat, fluffy blossoms on the acacia trees.

Around about April it starts to cool down and then *tjuntalpa* clouds may bring rain.

piriya-piriya
peer ee yah **peer** ee yah

mai wiyaringkupai
may **we** ah **ring** goo pay

kuli
coolie

marutjara
mar roo jah rah

utuwari
oo do worry

Anangu
ah nung oo

itjanu
ee jah noo

tjuntalpa
jawn dull pah

utuwaṟi
oo do worry

piriya-piriya
peer ee yah **peer** ee yah

wanitjunkupai
one ee **joon** goo pay

linga
ling ah

maḻu
mah loo

inuntji
in oon jee

Like *utuwaṟi* clouds they come from the south, and are carried first on a southerly wind; then as it gets cooler they are blown in on a westerly. These clouds sit low over the hills until late in the day. Then they might fade or go away, but they come back again, and they do this until it is *piriya-piriya* again.

When the cold time starts, many snakes and lizards go into hibernation. This is called *wanitjunkupai.* Occasionally it will warm up enough for them to come out for food, but they do not stay out long. The other animals and some lizards, such as the *linga* (central netted-dragon), do not hibernate when it is cold.

If the rain is good, then the time from Christmas to June is a really good growing time and everything is green. *Maḻu,* the red plains kangaroo, gets fat. Even after the grass dries out, they stay looking good because they eat the *inuntji* (blossom) on the acacia trees. But as it gets colder there is no green growth at all and the *inuntji* is finished. Then the wind comes in from the west and the kangaroos start to get skinny.

The coldest time of the year is called *wari.* Around July and August the nights are clear and freezing, and there is often frost and mist or dew in the morning. Most of the snakes and lizards are asleep now, and there is not much food around.

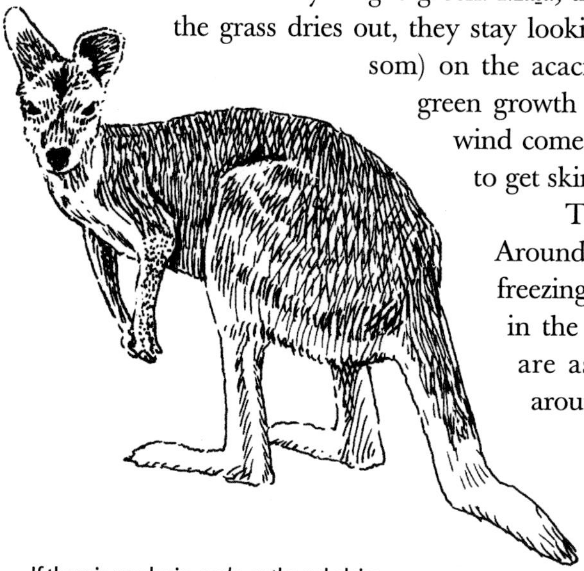

If there is good rain, *maḻu*, or the red plains kangaroo, thrives during the first half of the year.

After *wari* it is *piriya-piriya*, and everything gets going again. This is when the animals have their babies and there are plenty of flowers and fruit on the trees and bushes. Anangu look forward to this time because there is so much food to collect, such as seeds from grasses and shrubs. Seeds can be crushed and made into *latja*, an edible paste, and *nyuma*, a bread made from ground seeds and water and cooked in ashes. This time is also called *kaliny-kalinypa* after the honey grevillea which flowers around then. The nectar makes a lovely sweet drink which is very popular, especially with the children.

If the rains have been good, *maku* (witchetty grubs) are easy to find and *tjala* (honey ants) can be found close to the surface of the ground at the base of mulga trees. They are easy to dig up then. Also, *kurku* drips off the mulga. (*Kurku* is the red lac scale on the branches of mulga which

Top: Honey grevillea flower.
Centre: Elizabeth Wilson digs for witchetty grubs with her son Manu.
Bottom: *Maku*, or witchetty grubs, still in their roots.

latja
lah jah

nyuma
new mah

kaliny-kalinypa
cull in **cull** in pah

maku
mah goo

tjala
jah lah

kurku
cuckoo

tjaḻa
jah lah

mingkiri
ming gear ree

Aṉangu
ah nung oo

ailuru
ay loo roo

produce a sweet secretion.) Kids love this, and so do *tjaḻa*. It makes a good sweet drink, but it can also be eaten straight off the tree. It comes out of the crusty growth on the branches, and sometimes there is so much of it the tree shines, and the ground underneath the branches is wet.

Many animals, particularly *mingkiri*, mice and small marsupials, breed when there is plenty of food and soon they are running around everywhere. Sometimes there are so many that it is possible to collect billycans full of them from around the camp. Aṉangu have to tie their food in bags, and string it up in trees so that these *mingkiri* won't get at it.

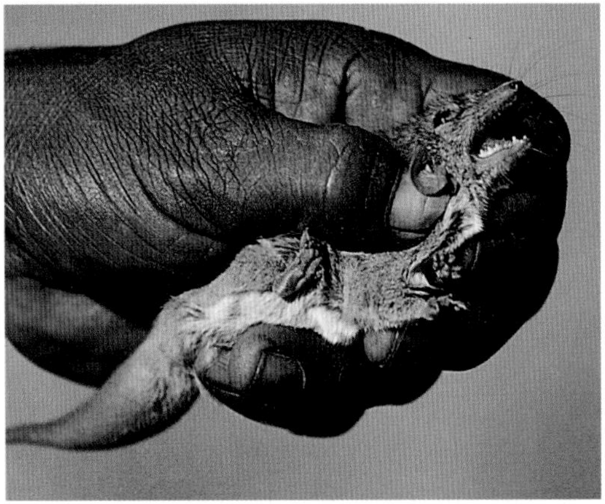

A mulgara, or *murtja*, which can be plentiful during *piriya-piriya,* is held by Edith Richards, a ranger at the park.

Ailuru – Drought

A lot depends on the rainfall. Sometimes there is plenty of rain, but sometimes it does not rain at all, and this can go on for years. Aṉangu call it *ailuru*, and this is the most difficult time. Plants and animals

Maureen Natjuna from the Mutitjulu Community digs for *tjala*, or honey ants.

have different ways of surviving. In dry times *tjala* move deep underground and digging them up becomes very hard work. *Tarkawara* (spinifex hopping-mice) store spinifex seeds and bush onions in their burrows so that they have food for these dry times, but many still die. Large animals – *malu* and *kalaya* (emu) – are able to move on. They can go a long way looking for food and in the past Anangu used to follow them.

In the olden days this was a difficult time for Anangu, because it meant having to travel great distances for food and water. That is one of the reasons people moved around so much. Anangu followed the food created by good rain and left a place when food and water became scarce.

There were more animals around then, but they are not here now. In the past these animals would come back after the dry times. However, since white people came some of them have not come back,

tarkawara
tucker worra

malu
mah loo

kalaya
kah lah yah

Anangu
ah nung oo

mitika
midi car

mala
mah lah

partjata
par jut ah

wintaru
win dah roo

such as the *mitika*, *mala*, *partjata* and *wintaru*. The Pi<u>r</u>anpa names for these animals are burrowing bettong, rufous hare-wallaby, western quoll and golden bandicoot.

A<u>n</u>angu do not really know why these animals disappeared, but some of the people around here remember when it happened.

During the 1930s, people were forced from their lands for many years by an extremely bad drought. When they returned, all of these animals, except for a few *ninu* (bilbies) and *wayu<u>t</u>a* (possums), had gone and they never returned.

Nobody really understands why this happened. Perhaps they moved away because there were too many changes to the country made by Pi<u>r</u>anpa, or because A<u>n</u>angu had moved off their traditional

The *mala*, or rufous hare-wallaby, is an animal that is now locally extinct.

country and were not able to maintain the Tjukurpa and look after the land. Perhaps it was because of the rabbits eating their food, or foxes and cats eating the animals that survived the drought. Many people, both Anangu and Piranpa, are talking about this these days, to find out where these animals went, and to bring them back if that is possible.

All these things are important to Anangu: rain and dry times, the cycles of the weather and how the animals and plants are managing. It all comes from Tjukurpa and Anangu must know it so that the land will survive.

Top: Alan Wilson, a senior member of the Mutitjulu Community, unearths a lizard for a watching Piranpa scientist.
Bottom: Anangu Ranger Andy Panpanalala Daeger, discusses a reptile with scientist Craig Martin.

Piranpa
peer un pah

Anangu
ah nung oo

ninu
nee noo

wayuta
why your dah

Tjukurpa
jook oor pah

Chapter 2

Tjanpi, tali munu pila

Spinifex, sandhills and sandplains

tjanpi
jarn bee

tali
tah lee

pila
bill ah

kiti
kee dee

waputi
wop or dee

Most of the country around Uluṟu is spinifex sandplains and sandhills. Aṉangu call the sandplains *pila* and the dunes *tali*. This is where most of the bush food and plenty of the animals can be found. As you drive around the park, particularly in the early morning or late afternoon, stop and look for these plants and animals or their tracks and burrows.

The most common plant is *tjanpi* (spinifex). There are many different types of spinifex, but one that Aṉangu use a lot is *tjanpi kiṯi*. *Kiṯi* is the resin from a type of spinifex and it is used to plug up holes and cracks in bowls and other things. Aṉangu also use it when they make their tools and weapons.

Many plants grow on the sandhills, and some of these make good food for both Aṉangu and animals. For example, the *waputi* (desert thryptomene) has a sweet nectar in its small flowers. This freezes on

A jewel beetle sips nectar from the flowers of the desert thryptomene.

walkalpa
woll gull pah

mut̲inka
more din gah

frosty nights, and An̲angu collect the nectar while it is still frozen by beating the bushes with a wooden bowl. However, another shrub, *walkalpa* (emu poison bush) is dangerous and should not be touched. It is very poisonous. An̲angu use it to hunt emus. The dried and crushed leaves are put in the water where emus come to drink. The poison slows them down, and then they are easy to kill.

Most hunting is done on the sandplains because not too many large animals live in the sandhills, and most of the small mammals that do live in them are also found down on the sandplains. But some lizards, like the *mut̲inka*, can be found on the dunes. *Mut̲inka* are small skinks with stripes going down their bodies and long tails. There are many different types of *mut̲inka*. You can tell them apart because they come in all different sizes and colours. An̲angu do not eat *mut̲inka*.

After rain, lots of frogs come out around the waterholes near Ulu̲ru and

Mut̲ingka, the small striped skink *Ctenotus quattuordecimlineatus*, pauses for a moment on a fallen desert oak cone.

Kata Tjuṯa. They also live on the side of sandhills which gets the rain, or the side the water runs down. They lie buried under the sand and then when the dune gets wet, they come out. They also live around waterholes.

There are other trees and bushes that grow on the sandplains apart from spinifex. There is *kurkaṟa* (desert oak), *waṯarka* (umbrella bush) and *muur-muurpa* (bloodwood). These trees are good for food and sometimes medicine. Sweet juice on the cones of *kurkaṟa*, and the gum on *muur-muurpa* is good for sores. Seeds from *waṯarka* can be crushed up and made into a paste to eat, but Aṉangu only eat this when there is not much food about. *Wakalpuka* (dead finish) seeds can also be eaten, once they've been ground up and mixed with water. *Nyii-nyii* (zebra finches) like the dead finish bush for nesting because it protects them with its spiky leaves. Other plants provide sweet nectar, such as *kaliny-kalinypa*

Two burrowing frogs mate after a long wait for rain, buried deep in the desert sand.

kurkaṟa
core kah rah

waṯarka
what ah kah

muur-muurpa
more more pah

wakalpuka
woggle booker

nyii-nyii
nyee nyee

kaliny-kalinypa
cull in **cull** in pah

witjinti
witch indy

mangata
mung ah dah

arnguli
ah noo lee

nyaru
nyah roo

kampurarpa
come poor rah pah

tarkawara
tucker worra

tjantjalka
jarn jull kah

(honey grevillea), and *witjinti* (corkwood tree). Animals and birds, as well as Anangu, love the fruit which grows on *mangata* and *arnguli*. These are the quondong and wild plum trees and are found on the sandplains, though they grow in other places as well.

Sandplains and sandhills covered with old spinifex are considered rubbish country. Anangu burn this. Burning cleans up the country. It also gets the bush food growing again, for people and for animals. As you drive around the park you will see where the country has been burnt and how the plants have grown up after recent fires or from burnings which have happened in the past. In cool weather you may see the smoke from patch burns which have been lit by Anangu and park staff. When the country is all burnt it is called *nyaru*. After rain, succulent plants sprout on the *nyaru*, such as *kampurarpa* (bush tomato and bush raisin) and edible seeds from grasses.

Some animals, such as *tarkawara*, the spinifex hopping-mouse, like to feed in *nyaru*, but others, such as *tjantjalka* (dragon lizards), need to live in spinifex areas and will move away from country that has been burnt.

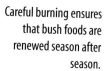

Careful burning ensures that bush foods are renewed season after season.

itjaritjari
eat jar eat jar ee

Tjukurpa
jook oor pah

tjuratja
jaw rah jah

Itjaritjari (marsupial mole)

Itjaritjari is a small blind marsupial which burrows around in the dunes and sandplains. It is one of the many Tjukurpa animals associated with the creation of Uluru. *Itjaritjari* spends most of its time underground and moves by digging a small tunnel which falls in behind it as it digs. If you sit still you can sometimes hear it digging underneath the sand. The tunnel rises and falls and travels in all directions. *Itjaritjari* often come up to the surface after rain, and you cannot mistake their tracks. They are not like any other animal's.

Itjaritjari eat small lizards and insects and sometimes *tjuratja*, sweet things such as honeydew, nectar and the sugary hard bits which you find on gum leaves. They also eat seeds, especially mulga seeds.

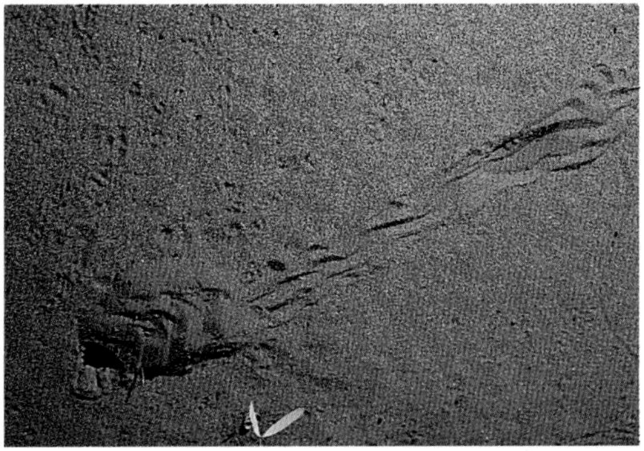

Above: The *itjaritjari* leaves a distinctive trail as its tunnel collapses behind it as it burrows through sand.
Left: A marsupial mole feeds on a gecko.

tarkawar̲a
tucker worra

katat̲a
kah dah dah

Tarkawar̲a **(spinifex hopping-mouse)**

Tarkawar̲a are mice with long legs, long ears and a long tufted tail. The females do not have pouches but have nipples on their belly to feed their babies. *Tarkawar̲a* belong to the sand-plains and dunes but during good seasons they will come up to the rocky areas and mulga country for a feed.

Tarkawar̲a live in large family groups in very deep burrows. The main entrance to the burrow is covered up with a big pile of sand and the passage is very steep. Tunnels lead off all over the place and there are lots of small holes for the mice to come in and go out of the burrow. These small holes are called *katat̲a*. They block these with pebbles and sand when they are not being used to stop predators from entering. These tunnels drop straight down so the mice can quickly get away from predators when they are above ground. They can also escape from inside the burrow by springing up out of the hole.

Inside the burrow there are special rooms for the babies. The mice make nests inside these rooms out of chewed spinifex. The little ones move out after they are weaned and start up new burrows. However, some will occasionally stay with their parents. The ones that stay do not

Spinifex hopping-mice emerge from their underground burrows at night to search for food.

tarkawara
tucker worra

nyaru
nyah roo

murtja
more jah

ailuru
ay loo roo

have their own babies until their parents die.

Tarkawara move burrow constantly to stay close to good food supplies. When they come out to feed they follow pathways they have made and this is one way to keep track of them. They like *nyaru* country, the regrowth after fire. There's more plants around then, more variety, and they scratch around for seeds and green leaves.

During *ailuru* (drought), *tarkawara* store food in their burrow and stay in the area until it rains and things grow again. You do not see many of them around during this time, and in fact many die. But after good rains they breed up again and you can see them running around at night. You might see them crossing the roads or, if you are camping at the Yulara camp ground, sometimes visiting the tents for food.

GETTING SCARCE

Murtja (mulgara)

Murtja are like mice, but a little bit bigger. They have a long nose, lots of small sharp teeth, and the end of their tail is a black tuft. The females have a pouch. They live in burrows and usually come out at night, but they also love to sunbake. Sometimes you can see the marks left in the sand where they have stretched out and basked in the sun. They have a

The *murtja*, or mulgara, prefers spinifex areas, where it can eat mulga and grass seeds and sometimes grasshoppers.

murtja
more jah

itjaritjari
eat jar eat jar ee

tjakuṟa
jah core rah

kuniya
coo nee ah

pila
bill ah

distinctive track and they sometimes create a shelter in spinifex to rest in while they are above ground.

Murtja are particular about the type of spinifex they live in. They do not like really old spinifex, nor do they like recently burnt areas, so it is important to burn the country properly.

They live on the sandplains and around the bottom of dunes, and also make their burrows in sandy areas on the edge of claypans and salt lakes. They like the same places as *itjaritjari, tjakuṟa* and *kuniya* (marsupial mole, giant desert skink and woma python).

Their burrows have a single entrance with a long straight tunnel and two very large rooms. When they are breeding, they build extra holes, tunnels and false entrances. Their nests are made of sticks and other bits and pieces. Sometimes *murtja* will re-dig old goanna burrows instead of making their own. The males often have two female partners and only breed once a year, unlike mice who do not have partners and, in good seasons, breed all year round.

There are not many *murtja* around now. You see more of them after a good rain but during the dry times they are hard to find. Often they die during these times because they are too small to move away. They used to be common around the park but they are not any more. The best place to look for them is in the *pila* or sandplain country between Yulara and the Park Entry Station.

kuniya
coo nee ah

tjakuṟa
jah core rah

murtja
more jah

iraṯi
ee rah dee

liru
leer roo

Kuniya (woma python)

Kuniya is a big snake, but it is not poisonous and Aṉangu can eat it. Like a lot of the animals around here it is an important part of the Tjukurpa for Uluṟu, but you will not find live ones in the rocks. *Kuniya* like to be by themselves, not with other *kuniya*, and they only live in certain places, such as on the sandplains where *tjakuṟa* and *murtja* live.

Kuniya eat meat and Aṉangu believe that they have an *iraṯi* (a power, killing magic) with which they 'sing' rabbits to death from a distance without having to touch them. They love rabbits whatever the size, from young kittens to adults. *Kuniya* swallow their prey whole. *Liru* (poisonous snakes) also have such power but it is in their poison and they have to bite their prey to kill it.

The female *kuniya* keeps her eggs in a little circular nest of grass, leaves and sticks. She wraps herself around the eggs until they hatch and stays with the babies until they grow up. In the Tjukurpa, the female *kuniya* makes a 'pocket' around her neck and she puts her eggs in this and carries them.

Kuniya, or the woma python, lives on spinifex sandplains where it often takes over rabbit burrows.

tjakuṟa
jah core rah

kuniya
coo nee ah

murtja
more jah

itjaritjari
eat jar eat jar ee

tjaḻiri
jah lee ree

lungkata
loong gah dah

GETTING SCARCE

Tjakuṟa (great desert skink)

The great desert skink, or *tjakuṟa*.

Aṉangu eat *tjakuṟa,* fat lizards with smooth scales. They start off with orange on their backs and yellow on their stomachs and these colours get stronger as they grow up. If you grab their long tail it breaks off easily.

They live on the sandplains and particularly like places that have been burnt and are getting some new growth. However they do not mind living in old spinifex. Like *kuniya,* they are only found in some places, usually in the same places that *murtja, kuniya* and *itjaritjari* live. They also live close to *tjaḻiri,* another edible skink.

Tjakuṟa make their own burrows, which are very large compared to their size and they are always fighting to protect their homes from other animals which try to steal them. The burrows often have many entrances and *tjakuṟa* leave a mound of droppings near the main entrance to mark it as their place. Sometimes they can be found in goanna burrows, especially after big rains, and other times they enlarge the holes of other lizards and move in there.

Tjakuṟa lay lots of eggs, around ten or so. They eat ants and move around at night and during the cooler part of the day. During the heat of the day they stay inside their burrow. They hibernate during the cold months, but when they hear the sound of rain and lightning, they come out. During dry times they stay in the same place and manage to stay alive, but they prefer good seasons when it rains.

Tjakuṟa and *tjaḻiri* are part of the same Tjukurpa story, the one about *lungkaṯa* (the blue-tongue lizard).

kalaya
kah lah yah

Anangu
ah nung oo

akalpa
ah call pah

***Kalaya* (emu)**

In the old days, Anangu and *kalaya* often travelled around the same places, moving from one waterhole to another. But *kalaya* do not stay around burnt country because there is not enough cover and wedge-tailed eagles take their chicks. Anangu know it is important not to burn country when *kalaya* are laying eggs or when there are little ones because it frightens them and they move away.

Kalaya lay nine to ten eggs, but not all at once. They will lay one egg, then a day or two later another one. So it takes a long time for all the eggs to be laid. The female lays the eggs but the male sits on them until they are hatched. *Kalaya* stay at the nest until the chicks are old enough to move on. This is a dangerous time for *kalaya*, because they are good to eat and their enemies can find them easily.

The chicks have striped feathers so that they can hide easily. But the adults also carry the chicks' dung away in their beaks, and put it a long way away from the nest so that there is no smell or sign of *kalaya* being there. This way the chicks can use their stripes to hide from eagles in the air and from dingoes and people on the ground.

Once the chicks are old enough, the family travels around. The chick which is striped and still travelling in a mob with its parents is called *akalpa*, while one of about the same age but travelling at a

The emu, or *kalaya*.

tjampuṉi
jum bore nee

paṯiny paṯinypa
pah din **pah** din
pah

distance from its family is called *tjampuṉi*. This particular chick is likely to be caught and eaten.

Paṯiny-paṯinypa (Burton's snake-lizard)

Paṯiny-paṯinypa are small lizards that look like snakes but are not, because they have tiny little feet. They have a long pointy nose, a divided tongue, a wide mouth and their colour varies depending on where they live. And they live all over the place.

They are found in shallow burrows under the spinifex on the sandplains and dunes, but they also burrow under fig trees, among the rocks. Because their burrows are so shallow *paṯiny-paṯinypa* get burnt when there is a fire. During droughts they stay underground and only come out after rain, when the ground is wet.

Hawks, perenties, snakes and many other things like to eat *paṯiny-paṯinypa,* so they stay in their burrows during the day when the goannas and these other animals are hunting, and then come out at night. *Paṯiny-paṯinypa* eat seeds, figs that have fallen off the trees, other small lizards and sometimes ants. Sometimes they can be aggressive, particularly if you find them in honey-ant burrows eating the eggs. Often at night

Burton's snake-lizard, or *paṯiny-paṯinypa*.

paṯiny paṯinypa
pah din **pah** din
pah

muḻutiṉpa
more loo din pah

puḻṯanpa
paul dun bah

liru
leer roo

inma
in mah

mitika
midi car

when they are not hunting they will climb up onto the top of spinifex hummocks and call out, but they stop this when the sun comes up.

When they come to lay their eggs, *paṯiny-paṯinypa* prepare a nest in a very deep burrow under the spinifex. They stay with the eggs until they hatch. This is the way some snakes do it too.

There are other lizards like snakes related to *paṯiny-paṯinypa*. One is called *muḻutiṉpa*, but it moves more slowly, has no feet, is a different colour and lives in different places. The other is called *puḻṯanpa* and lives in the sand dunes.

These three lizards are related to the *liru* in the Tjukurpa, but they are not poisonous. There is an *inma* or ceremony for *paṯiny-paṯinypa* at Ininti Rockhole on the north side of Uluṟu. A long time ago, according to the Tjukurpa, *paṯiny-paṯinypa* had legs and fangs and could bite. But then something happened and it turned it into a legless, fangless animal, but different to a snake. It still has very small feet, so even though its tongue is divided, it is not a snake.

LOCALLY EXTINCT

Mitika (burrowing bettong)

Before Piṟanpa arrived there were more animals around Uluṟu. Many of them went away and have not come back. No-one knows why, and they have either died or gone somewhere else to live. Big animals

Before European occupation, the *mitika*, or burrowing bettong, was found on spinifex plains, creekbanks and salt lakes. It is now locally extinct.

mingkiri
ming gear ree

mitika
midi car

wayuṯa
why your dah

tjiraṉka
jeer run gar

and the little ones, like kangaroos and *mingkiri*, have managed all right, but many of the middle-sized ones have finished up. They were about the size of a rabbit or a cat and were good food for Aṉangu. They are still important Tjukurpa animals. One of these was the *mitika*.

Mitika were large fat animals with a short tail and big ears and their tracks were similar to those of rock wallabies. They used to live on the sandplains, in creek banks and around salt lakes. You could see their tracks on the sand and they dug large burrows, especially in creek banks. They came out at night and were often found around the same places as *wayuṯa* (brushtail possums). Aṉangu would hunt both *mitika* and *wayuṯa* at night with dogs.

Mitika disappeared from this country around thirty, maybe fifty, years ago, but people are reminded of them from the Tjukurpa and from what older people remember.

> *When I was a child I saw mitika at Mantaṟur and Piṟupakaḻaṟinytja [rocky ranges south-west of Kata Tjuṯa]. We hunted them with dogs, dug them out of their burrows and grabbed them. I was* tjiraṉka *[pre-adolescent] and we used to get them all the time. They are finished up here now but they might be somewhere else.*
>
> Senior informant
> Uluṟu–Kata Tjuṯa National Park Vertebrate Fauna Survey

LOCALLY EXTINCT

Mala (rufous hare-wallaby)

Another animal which has gone from here is the *mala. Mala* are a small wallaby that used to live around Uluṟu and are an important part of the Tjukurpa. They lived in the sand dunes. They do not dig burrows, but sit under the spinifex hummocks.

In good seasons Aṉangu used to be able to hunt them in large numbers but during droughts there were not so many – just pairs of males and females together. Like *mitika* they disappeared from this country a long time ago.

The *mala*, or rufous hare-wallaby, is one of the animals that has disappeared from the park.

mala
mah lah

mitika
midi car

Chapter 3

Wanar̲i

Mulga country

Another place in the park where there are lots of animals and different plants is *wanar̲i*, or mulga woodlands. *Wanar̲i* is a bush or little tree, but sometimes it can grow tall as well. It is also called mulga, and they all grow together like a woodland. An̲angu get a lot of bush food from here; also, the wood is very hard and makes good tools and weapons, and old people use mulga branches to make a fire.

The ground in this country is hard and can be stony, so it floods quickly after a big rain, and can get very boggy. In between patches of mulga you can find claypans. After rain these claypans fill up with water. This is called *tjintjir̲a*, and is good for animals to drink at for a while, but the water does not last long.

During dry times, not much grows on the ground in mulga country. Spinifex might grow there, if the soil is sandy. But after a big rain all sorts of grasses and small plants grow up underneath the trees. The mulga begins flowering and may be laden with seeds. An̲angu collect these seeds to make flour for *nyuma*, a seed cake, and *latja*, a paste An̲angu eat. Seeds and

wanar̲i
one ah ree

An̲angu
ah nung oo

tjintjir̲a
jin jeer ah

nyuma
new mah

latja
lah jah

Honey ants in their nest, deep in the desert sand under a stand of mulga trees.

pakuṯa
park or dar

parka-parka
barker **bark**er

tjaḻa
jah lah

muya-muya
moo yah **moo** yah

puraṟa
poor rah rah

fruit, good ones to eat, grow on the mulga and other trees and bushes as well.

There are several different types of mulga, and Aṉangu know the different food which comes from them. For example, insects make a thing like a small apple on the *pakuṯa* (horse mulga). This one is good to eat, but there is another one on a different sort of mulga which is not edible. Sometimes another plant, called *parka-parka,* grows all over the mulga. Piṟanpa call this mistletoe. It makes a sweet fruit that children love. In the old days the women would leave the children eating this while they went about digging for *tjaḻa.*

Tjaḻa (honey ant)

Tjaḻa is one of the really good foods that live in mulga country. They make a sweet honey which Aṉangu eat straight from the ant, or add to damper. These *tjaḻa* start making their nest after rain and dig it deep into the ground with many tunnels and different sections. These nests are always found around the bottom of a full-grown mulga, just under where the water drips off the leaves. Usually the burrows are on the shady side of the bush.

Tjaḻa are the ants that contain the honey. They are the mothers of the workers, and cannot move around. They cling to the ceiling of their chambers where other ants feed them on the sweet juice and nectar from the mulga and other trees such as corkwoods and emu bush. The eggs and the baby ants are kept deep down in the nest. The baby ants get fed *muya-muya,* the grubs which live on mulga leaves. When there is not enough food around, particularly during dry times, the *puraṟa* (worker ants)

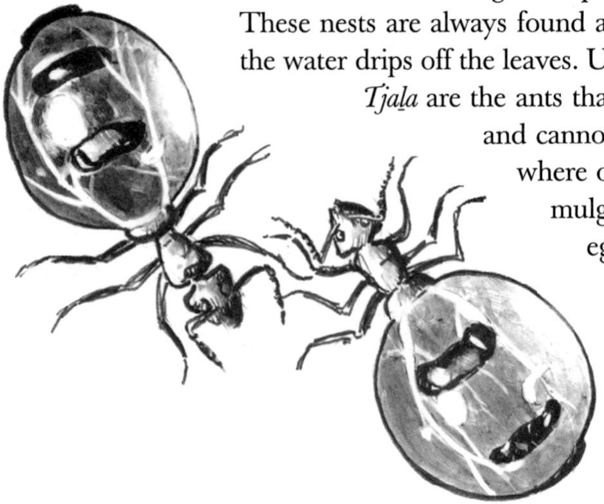

make *tjaḻa* cough up what is in their stomachs to feed the young *tjaḻa* and the workers.

To find the nest, Aṉangu search for worker ants among the leaves and sticks on the ground, and then follow them back to the nest. Sometimes by scraping back the rubbish on the ground you can see the ants coming and going out of the nest. When digging up the nest it is important not to destroy the places where *tjaḻa* are. It is also important to look out for scorpions resting in the tunnels. To avoid breaking the chambers, the tunnels are dug from the side, not from the top down. Aṉangu follow the tunnels by looking at the colour and feel of the earth and by using a fine stick to figure out which direction they go in. It is hard work and may take several hours to dig out enough *tjaḻa* for everyone to eat. Usually women do this work.

Tjaḻa are very delicate, and can break easily in your hand. In the olden days, the grandmothers used to make carrying boxes of dough made from ground grass seeds to carry them back to camp. These days they use flour tins or billies.

Digging for honey ants.

ninu
nee noo

tjaḻa
jah lah

mitika
midi car

mala
mah lah

maḻu
mah loo

kanyaḻa
carn yah lah

LOCALLY EXTINCT

Ninu (bilby)

A̲nangu are not the only ones who like eating *tjaḻa*. Animals like *ninu* also love them. Like *mitika* (burrowing bettong) and *mala* (hare-wallaby), *ninu* used to be very common around here. They are a bit like a rabbit, with long ears and long pointed noses, but they also have long tails which are fluffy at the end. They move around at night and live in great long burrows. The burrows go round and round and are very deep. *Ninu* love honey ants. Sometimes the old women would dig out a honey-ant nest only to find a *ninu* there already. When this happened they might say, "Let's eat the bilby, not the honey ants, as the bilby has already got the honey ants inside it."

The bilby, or *ninu*, are extinct in the park, but A̲nangu still know of their habits.

Maḻu (red plains kangaroo)

Maḻu are the red plains kangaroos. They are found in the mulga when good feed is around. *Kanyaḻa* (euro, hill kangaroo) might also come into the mulga but only if it is close

ulpuṟu
ool pour roo

maḻu
mah loo

kanyaḻa
carn yah lah

to rocky hill country. You can find *maḻu* in the places A<u>n</u>angu call *ulpuṟu*. This is a place where animals may have slept or rested. It is an open, dusty place with lots of grass and where the wind can come through easily. There is no spinifex or prickles. Kangaroos do not like prickles. Sometimes it has steep ditches or gullies as well.

Maḻu are important animals of the Tjukurpa. They are also good meat for people.

When it is hot, *maḻu* stay in the bush for shade, but when it is cold they live in the open and come together in groups to feed. A single kangaroo might travel a long way to find food and then come back. The others will smell grass on its breath and follow it to wherever the good food is.

Maḻu stay in places with green grass and herbs. As long as the feed is green and moist they do not need water. You will not find them in rocky hills or where water runs down. They stay away from creeks because they do not like boggy ground and, unlike *kanyaḻa*, they do not like rocky areas either. When they think that a place might be boggy, they feel the ground with their front feet to make sure the ground is firm before moving on to it.

During dry times, *maḻu* will travel long distances to find food and water, then return to the mulga to rest.

Maḻu, or the red plains kangaroo, forage for food on a sandplain.

wayuṯa
why your dah

mitika
midi car

Wayuṯa (brushtail possum)

There are not too many *wayuṯa* around now. In the olden days, Aṉangu used to eat them, and they are still very important in the Tjukurpa. They used to live at Uluṟu and Kata Tjuṯa and there are still some living west of here towards Docker River. Once they were all over the place in trees, caves, creeks, everywhere. They live inside dry hollow trees and where there are no hollow trees they use caves, or empty space in termite mounds or sometimes they nest in *mitika* and rabbit burrows. Sometimes they would be found in hollowed-out desert oaks. One of their favourite trees to sleep in are river red gums.

Wayuṯa do not come out during the day, but at night they come out and eat the blossoms of flowering mulga, ironwoods and bloodwood trees. They climb down onto the ground, moving around all the different plants, eating fruits, seed and leaves as well as the flowers. They feed all night, and travel around looking for food and then they sleep near to where they find it. *Wayuṯa* will drink water but can live where there is no water around.

The brushtail possum, or *wayuṯa*.

Maybe bushfires killed a lot of *wayuṯa* because they cannot travel very quickly on the ground. Their feet are not much good for walking or running on the ground. After fire,

wayuṯa
why your dah

maḻu
mah loo

wayuṯa still feed on the mulga and ironwood trees rather than on all the different plants which spring up after burning.

During drought, *wayuṯa* live on bloodwood leaves and buds from the river red gums. In good times they feed a lot from mulga, but mulga dies out during drought. Because there's not much food around in dry times, a good many *wayuṯa* end up together in the same place, moving to where there is food. Here they spread out among the green trees and sometimes the family will go a long way in different directions looking for food.

Wayuṯa live in families, with the male staying with the female and young possums. Each family has its own place for sleeping. Sometimes a single adult male might be found in a hollow tree, or just a female with little ones. The young possums move out and set themselves up in a new place once they grow up. A family group may have an extra adult female, other than the mother, but never another male, even if it is a son. Sometimes you might see a couple of males fighting over a female. Like the *maḻu*, they don't fight over food or territory but they do fight over females.

When there were lots of *wayuṯa*, A<u>n</u>angu would catch maybe four or five every night. At Kata Tjuṯa, boys would feel around inside the hollow parts of a tree looking for them. To scare them out of trees, A<u>n</u>angu would chop a hole in the side of the tree and light a fire inside it. That would smoke them out. When the animal ran out they'd hit it with a stick, and it would fall to the ground. Then a dog would grab it so the hunter could kill it. Often after cutting out the hole the boys might find not just one but three or more possums in the tree.

mingkiri
ming gear ree

anula
ah nool lah

wiltjinypa
will jin bah

murtja
more jah

tarkawara
tucker wurra

katata
kah dah dah

Mingkiri **(small mice and marsupials)**

Mingkiri is an Anangu name for some small mice and marsupials. There are many other names for little animals: *anula, wiltjinypa, murtja* and *tarkawara*, but *mingkiri* is the name used mostly these days. These animals are all the same, but a little bit different as well.

Piranpa have many names for these animals as well. Some of these are sandy inland mouse, desert mouse, house mouse, wongai ningaui, Ooldea dunnart, hairy-footed dunnart and the lesser hairy-footed dunnart. But even though Anangu call them all *mingkiri*, they know they are different animals and can tell them apart by how they look and act. For example, dunnarts might have a fat tail and mice have a thin tail. As well, dunnarts are different to mice because they have many small sharp teeth rather than two large front teeth, and female dunnarts have a pouch, while mice have nipples on their stomach. However,

Top: The desert mouse, *Pseudomys desertor.*
Bottom: A ningaui, *Ningaui ridei,* eats a military dragon.

Top: A house mouse, *Mus musculus*.
Bottom: The sandy inland mouse, *Pseudomys hermannsburgensis*, eats a grasshopper.

there are many more mice around than dunnarts and usually, when A<u>n</u>angu talk about *mingkiri*, they mean the mice, not the dunnarts.

All *mingkiri* make burrows and love to dig. They look after their babies really well, making sure the burrows are well built, comfortable and safe. They make their burrows with one main hole, which is covered over, and a number of small holes they can jump up through. These 'pop-up' holes, called *kata<u>t</u>a*, are closed off a little way down when the mice are inside or when the adults go out looking for food, leaving the babies behind. This way snakes and goannas cannot get into the burrow. The main burrow is shallow and has quite a few rooms branching off it. Sometimes there is a second lot of rooms branching off from the first lot. *Mingkiri* might have their babies and look after them in these other rooms. They make their nests from chewed grass and lots of families live in the same set of burrows.

All the different types of mice have more or less the same sort of burrow, but there are some differences. For example, *tarkawa<u>r</u>a* make very deep burrows with larger *kata<u>t</u>a* or pop-up holes.

Mingkiri are found everywhere from rocky areas to the mulga country, sand dunes and sandplains. When they are out looking for food, they like the spinifex areas which grow up after

mingkiri
ming gear ree

ngapaḻa
nah pah lah

ngiyaṟi
nee yah ree

langka
loong gah

burning, though they prefer the older spinifex areas for making their burrows. *Mingkiri* will move long distances from their burrows to feed. They eat all the same plants and seeds that people like. They like to eat bush onions and where there are plenty of them, *mingkiri* collect and store them in their burrows. Sometimes they eat grasshoppers and moths but most of the time they eat plant food.

Mingkiri can breed very rapidly and during good seasons there are too many of them, but then they die during droughts because they are too little and cannot move away to better country.

Some *mingkiri* have gone from around Uluṟu. One kind used to live around Wingellina (or Irrunytju, far west of Kata Tjuṯa in Western Australia), and maybe they lived on the edges of Lake Amadeus as well, or at least around the salt pans. They liked soft ground. But they are not around here any more.

Ngapaḻa (dwarf bearded dragon)
You can find *ngapaḻa* in both spinifex and mulga country. These are different to other lizards because the mothers take special care of their young, instead of just leaving them. Some other animals, such as *ngiyaṟi* (thorny devil) and *langka*

The dwarf bearded dragon, or *ngapaḻa*, eats grasshoppers, flies, ants and beetles.

piṟurpa
peer roo pah

papangaurpa
pah pung hour pah

(blue-tongue lizard), just forget about their babies. The female *ngapaḻa* digs a deep burrow for her eggs and will sometimes dig several burrows until she is satisfied that she has made a good one. Then she lays her eggs, about nine of them, and covers them over carefully and goes away. When they start to hatch she comes back and opens the burrow to let the baby lizards out.

Piṟurpa (tree-living gecko)

Piṟurpa are geckoes that live in trees, including the spiny-tailed gecko. These have big toes for climbing, small eyes, and usually live under the bark. The spiny-tailed geckoes are bigger and more aggressive than geckoes which live on the ground. These ground geckoes are called *papangaurpa.* They stand taller and have longer bodies and tails, but their eyes and head are smaller.

Piṟurpa are often found in desert oaks, which grow on the sandplains and in mulga country. Some *piṟurpa* lay two or three eggs in a hole under spinifex at night while others lay four, maybe five, eggs under the bark of a tree. *Piṟurpa* eat flies and ants that crawl up the tree. Sometimes they move around from one place to another. They hibernate during the cold months but come out again on warm summer nights. They will move around during the cooler parts of the day but not when it is hot. They don't travel too far because of predators. Cats, snakes and goannas like to eat them, and if a fire comes through then they get burnt with the tree.

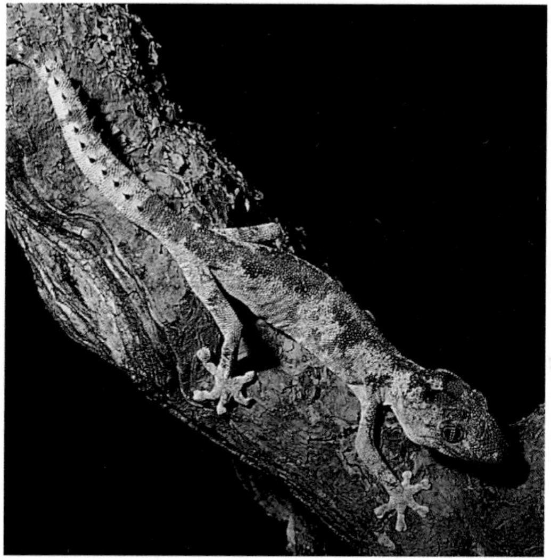

The spiny-tailed gecko, or *piṟurpa*, lives in trees.

puli
bully

kanyala
carn yah lah

Chapter 4

Puli
Rocky areas

Walking quietly along the tracks in the rocky hilly areas around Uluru and Kata Tjuta is probably the best way to see animals in the park. *Kanyala* (euro) can often be seen in the distance and sometimes jump off the tracks early in the morning or late in the afternoon. That is when you will see a lot of the lizards and birds as well.

Not all the animals live among the rocks. There are lots that live in the gullies and big trees as well as beside the creeks – reptiles, mice and small marsupials. Sometimes they will come out and scratch around the rocks for food, especially after a good rain. But then they go back to the softer, sandier places and the trees for their

Mt Olga Gorge a day after rain. Creeks and gullies in the park fill quickly after rain.

apar̲a
ah pah rah

mingkul̲pa
ming gall pah

wayut̲a
why your dah

il̲i
ear lee

burrows and nests. There are also birds which turn up after good rains but then go away again when the water dries up.

There are many plants around Ulur̲u and Kata Tjut̲a that are different from those on the sandplains and in the mulga. An̲angu use a lot of them for making tools and weapons as well as for food. For example, the sweet sugary things on the leaves of *apar̲a* (Pir̲anpa call these river red gums) are lovely to eat. Also An̲angu find little grubs in the roots to eat, and they burn the bark to mix it with *mingkul̲pa* (native tobacco). The roots from *apar̲a* are good for making bowls. *Wayut̲a* (brushtail possums) used to live in the old trees, but they are gone from around Ulur̲u now.

Il̲i (wild fig) are important in the Tjukurpa. An̲angu must look after these trees and see that they are not burnt or hurt. They have red

Mingkul̲pa, or native tobacco.

The bush raisin, or *kampur̲arpa*.

Il̲i, or the wild fig.

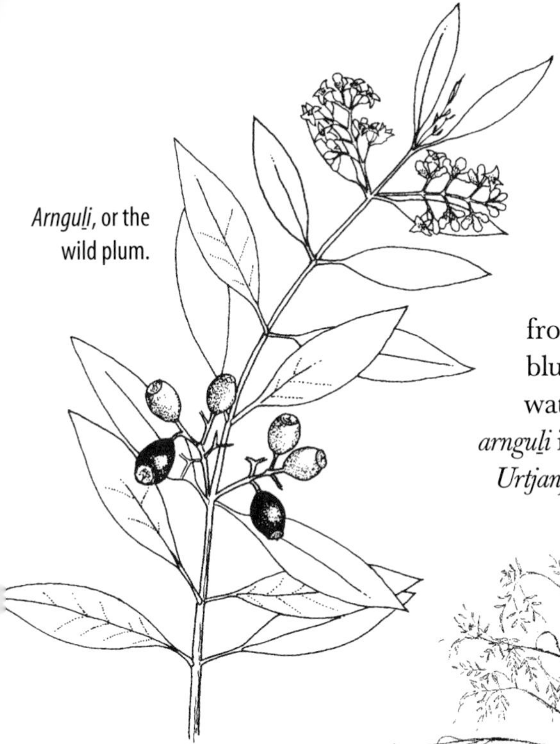

Arnguḻi, or the wild plum.

fruit that Aṉangu either pick off the tree and eat straight away or crush when they dry off to make a paste.

Arnguḻi is another fruit Aṉangu eat straight from the tree. These are wild plums, and are little bluey-black fruit. If they dry out Aṉangu soak them in water to make them swell up again. The wood from *arnguḻi* is good for carving.

Urtjanpa, the spear bush, is good for making spears. The branches are all bent on the bushes but Aṉangu chop them off one by one and straighten them out by

arnguḻi
ah noo lee

urtjanpa
or jun pah

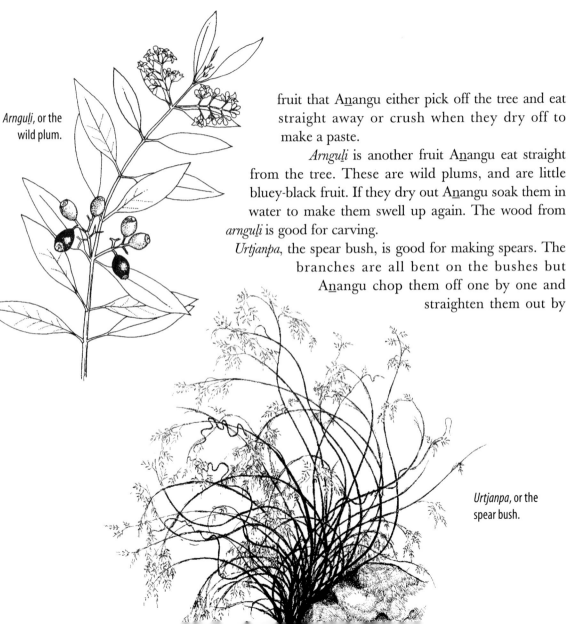

Urtjanpa, or the spear bush.

waru
worroo

mirilyirilyi
mee rill **yee** rill **yee**

ngin̲taka
nin dah kah

kanyal̲a
carn yah lah

arutju
a roo joo

tjilkamata
jill gah mah dah

heating them over the fire. The women use the little twigs from this bush to make spinning frames for hair and fur.

Lots of animals and birds live in the spinifex and rocks around Ulur̲u and Kata Tjut̲a. There used to be *waru*, rock wallabies, but these have become locally extinct. *Mirilyirilyi* (fairy wrens and dusky grasswrens) are found nesting near these rocky areas. It is a good place to find *ngin̲taka* (perentie), as well as *kanyal̲a, arutju* and *tjilkamat̲a.*

The fat-tailed antechinus, or *arutju*, prefers rocky areas.

Arutju (fat-tailed antechinus)

Arutju look a little like a small kangaroo, but more like a mouse. They have a fat tail and a long nose. Pir̲anpa scientists call them fat-tailed antechinus. The females have pouches. They live in the rocky areas, particularly in the cracks

murtja
more jah

mingkiri
ming gear ree

kanyaḻa
carn yah lah

between the boulders. They also live under boulders in holes, or where they scratch a bit of sand away. They make nests with grass. Around Uluṟu they live in among the big boulders at the bottom of the Rock, as well as up on top.

Arutju like to sunbake in the afternoon and often come out before dark to play. During very dry years they do not move away, they just stay put. However the family groups split up and live separately. A lot of them die during these times.

In the Tjukurpa, *arutju* are related to *murtja* (mulgara) and *mingkiri*, as well as *maḻu* (red plains kangaroo).

Kanyaḻa (euro, hill kangaroo)

Kanyaḻa are smaller than *maḻu* and they have rougher hair. They stay close to *puḻi* areas, but you might find them down on the sandplains as well. When they are chased by dingoes or Aṉangu, they seek refuge in rocky areas. Unlike *maḻu*, they can go anywhere as they do not mind boggy ground and will hop up and down the creekbeds.

The euro, or *kanyaḻa*, prefers rocky areas and gullies.

However, while *maḻu* can often get enough moisture from eating grass, *kanyaḻa* do need drinking water.

There are not too many *kanyaḻa* at Uluṟu these days, and these live at Tjukatjapi and Waṟayuki (registered sacred sites on the northern and western sides of Uluṟu), moving around to Ininti Rockhole and Kaṉtju Gorge for water. There are plenty of *kanyaḻa* at Kata Tjuṯa.

Tjilkamaṯa (echidna)

Aṉangu usually find *tjilkamaṯa* by looking for their droppings and diggings around Uluṟu and Kata Tjuṯa, but you can also sometimes find them out on the sandplains. There are usually two of them together. In the rocky areas, they are mainly in among the

The echidna, or *tjilkamaṯa*.

tjilkamaṯa
jill gah mah dah

kanyaḻa
carn yah lah

boulders and spinifex.

If you give *tjilkamaṯa* a fright they will roll up into a ball. They are not much good for eating because they are too fat, and only have little steaks, however, in times of need they are eaten. A<u>n</u>angu hunt them with spears; they are very slow and cannot get away once they are caught. There is a special way to prepare *tjilkamaṯa*, in keeping with the Tjukurpa. After they have been cleaned up properly they are put on hot ashes to bake. When they are a little bit cooked, A<u>n</u>angu scrape the spines off their back with the stone end of a throwing stick.

putukalya
put do gull yah

tjuntalpi
jawn dull pee

Putukalya (dragon lizard)

Putukalya is a small, spotted, red rock dragon that can change colour depending on its background. There are plenty of them around both Uluru and Kata Tjuta in rocky areas and on the flat open hard ground. *Putukalya* burrow into the sand under small rocks and eat mosquitoes, flies and ants. There is one very small ant that they particularly like.

Tjuntalpi (long-nosed dragon)

Tjuntalpi have a yellow stomach and a long tail. They move quickly and if suddenly frightened they run on their hind legs. They can be quite aggressive. They live all over the place and you can often find them up trees or bushes or among the rocks and sticks and leaves beside creekbeds.

They do all their hunting during the day and then sleep on the ground at night. Goannas like to eat *tjuntalpi* and *tjuntalpi*

Top: The *putukalya*, or lined earless dragon.
Bottom: The *tjuntalpi*, or long-nosed dragon.

tjuntalpi
jawn dull pee

aralapalpalpa
ah rull ah **paul** paul pah

wakalpuka
woggle booker

like to eat small skinks. They climb up trees hunting for geckoes, which escape them by staying under the bark.

Unlike many other lizards which hibernate during the cold months, *tjuntalpi* stay awake all winter. They lay five to ten eggs in a special burrow. The eggs hatch in early summer. Young *tjuntalpi* are slow growers, taking maybe one or two years before they are full grown. But then they live for a long time. You can tell how old they are by the length of their tail. A small-tailed *tjuntalpi* will be a young one.

Aralapalpalpa (crested pigeon)

Aralapalpalpa are everywhere, and they move around all the time. They peck about on the ground for grass seeds and seeds from *wakalpuka* (dead finish wattle). *Aralapalpalpa* make a nest in trees and lay two whitish-blue eggs. When the eggs hatch the parents and babies stay living together in a group.

Crested pigeons share a waterhole with *nyii nyii*, or zebra finches.

ikarka
ee kah kah

Ikarka **(western bowerbird)**

Ikarka is a bird which likes to live in among the rocks. It can be seen at Kata Tjuṯa and used to be at Uluṟu. It may still be there, north of Ikari, but no-one has seen any for some time.

Ikarka have a variety of calls and mimic other birds. They can laugh a little bit like a kingfisher and whistle as well. *Ikarka* make a shelter that is hidden in the scrub. The males and females build and decorate their shelter with black and white stones, glass and tin. When they breed they put the eggs in the shelter. They need water for drinking and will eat anything, including flies, but they really like wild figs.

The western bowerbird, or *ikarka*.

puntaru
porn da roo

Puntaru **(little button-quail)**

Puntaru is a small fat bird which runs around on the ground in the scrub and is often frightened out of the grass when you are walking around Uluru or Kata Tjuta. It is brown and has a short tail, but no crest.

Puntaru makes its nest in a hole on the ground and sits on small brown speckled eggs. It stores seeds in its throat.

The little button quail, or *puntaru*.

Chapter 5

Manta aṯunymankupai

Looking after country

manta
marn dah

aṯunymankupai
ah doon **marn** goo pay

nyaṟuni
nyah roo nee

Tjukurpa
jook oor pah

Aṉangu know a lot about country. Not just what animals do and where plants grow, but why they live the way they do and how they are related to each other and to the ancestral beings. This is part of the Tjukurpa. The Tjukurpa makes rain happen and tells Aṉangu when and how plants will grow, and where animals will be when they are needed for hunting. This knowledge has been passed down through the generations. It helps people live on the land and helps the country to stay alive.

There are certain people who know about how the country was made, and how the spirits behave, and there are special ways of learning it. It is very important that only the right people learn it, at the right time. If the wrong people are given this information, it breaks the Tjukurpa. That is why there are many things Aṉangu cannot tell other people. This is part of Aṉangu Law, and must be respected.

Nyaṟuni – Burning off

One of the ways Aṉangu look after country is through burning. Fires, whether lit by people or started by lightning, big ones or small ones, are part of the Tjukurpa.

The country is not burnt in just any way. Aṉangu are taught by their grandparents the proper way to burn, according to the Tjukurpa. Certain places, such as sacred sites and trees such as fig trees, should not be burnt because of their association with the Tjukurpa. The area around these trees is often burned to protect them. These sites are protected and

An area of Uluṟu–Kata Tjuṯa National Park is burned to ensure regeneration of important plants and animals.

mingkiri
ming gear ree

kal̲aya
kah lah yah

mal̲u
mah loo

An̲angu
ah nung oo

Pir̲anpa
peer un pah

nyar̲u
nyah roo

Tjunguringkula
joong or ring coo lah

waakaripai
wah curry pah

at the same time show others that the land is being properly cared for.

Burning old spinifex – the rubbish stuff – and sometimes mulga, helps grow food for animals and people and makes it easier to walk around the place. *Mingkiri* and many of the larger animals like the country being burned because they eat the same seeds and things as An̲angu and get plenty of food when it starts growing again.

The Tjukurpa shows An̲angu how animals will be with fire and burnt country. For example, some dragon lizards and other small animals don't like the ground after it's been burnt. They go away for a while, and then come back when the spinifex has grown again. Some animals, such as the spinifex hopping-mouse, like it both ways. They move into the burned areas to feed and then return to safety in the large unburnt spinifex hummocks where they have their burrows. *Kal̲aya* and *mal̲u* (emu and kangaroo) do not like freshly burnt country but come back to it after rain has brought on the green feed. Most animals and birds love the green feed near water.

Before Pir̲anpa came, there weren't big bushfires because the country had always been properly looked after by An̲angu and such fires did not occur. After Pir̲anpa arrived, An̲angu were forced to move away or were discouraged from looking after country in the old way, by patch burning. That was when An̲angu first started to see the huge bushfires that have killed off the country, in summers after years of good rainfall. When the first Pir̲anpa started burning, An̲angu were very worried because white people did not know the proper way to burn, nor did they know where the sacred places were and so they burnt places that should have been left alone.

An̲angu usually burn in the cool times or after good rains so that the fires can be controlled and the country can grow up after the spring and summer rains. Fires lit during heavy frost times do not burn well and patches of spinifex are left around the country. This way the fires do not get too big and at the same time they leave a bit of shelter and food behind for the animals. Anangu do not usually light fires in summer – most summer fires are caused by lightning.

Sometimes Anangu light small fires, sometimes big ones which might burn for days. Sometimes the fires will go out, other times they may keep going, moving quite fast. Anangu would follow them, keep them going, have a rest, and then keep them going again for a long way until the clouds built up and it rained.

It is important to burn when it is cool and there is no wind, or only a little wind, so that the fire moves slowly. If the wind makes the fire burn too quickly the animals cannot escape and they get burnt. If fire moves more slowly the animals feel the ground getting hot and go into their burrows. Then when the fire is finished they come up and move around in the *nyaru* (burnt-out country).

Anangu are teaching Piranpa staff the right way with fire and so now the country in the park is burnt properly.

Tjunguringkula waakaripai – Working together

Another way Anangu and Piranpa staff and scientists are working together is by looking for some of those animals that are not around much any more, such as *wayuta*, *murtja*, *itjarit-jari*, *tjakura* and one of the *mirilyirilyi*, the one the scientists call striated grasswren. When people know where these animals and birds are, they will work out ways to look after them and get their numbers up so that there will be plenty of them again.

Because Anangu know so much about the animals in the park, they play a very important role by telling scientists where animals live, what their nests look like, what they feed on, and how to find them by looking at tracks. This helps Piṟanpa understand how the animals and birds live, especially during droughts.

The management of Uluṟu–Kata Tjuṯa National Park is the joint responsibility of Aṉangu and the Australian Nature Conservation Agency (now Parks Australia). For this joint management to be successful, it is important for the Piṟanpa staff to learn and respect Aṉangu knowledge and their way of looking after the country. Aṉangu are learning some of the Piṟanpa ways too, such as using wildlife survey equipment, so that everybody can look after the country together.

We hope that this book has given you a better understanding of how Aṉangu care for their country and that it helps you see the country in a new way.

Pitjantjatjara/Yankunytjatjara wordlist

(P) or (Y) indicates a word specific to Pitjantjatjara or Yankunytjatjara

ailuru	drought conditions
akaḻpa	emu chick or young
Aṉangu	Aboriginal person or Aboriginal people
anula	?long-haired rat, *Rattus villosissimus,* ?Forrest's mouse, *Leggadina forresti*
apara (Y), itara (P)	river red gum, *Eucalyptus camaldulensis* var. *obtusa*
araḻapaḻpaḻpa	crested pigeon, *Ocyphaps lophotes*
arnguli (P), kupata (Y)	wild plum, *Santalum lanceolatum*
arutju	fat-tailed antechinus, *Pseudantechinus macdonnellensis*
ikarka	western bowerbird, *Chlamydera guttata*
ili	fig tree, *Ficus platypoda*
inma	ceremony
inuntjï	fresh plant growth, blossoms; the time of year when acacias blossom profusely, typically after summer rains, around January to March
iraṯi	killing magic, deadly magic weapon
itjanu	lush green country; verdant
itjaritjari	marsupial mole, *Notoryctes typhlops*
kaḻaya (Y), *tjakipiri* (P)	emu, *Dromaius novaehollandiae*
kaliny-kalinypa	honey grevillea, *Grevillea eriostachya;* also the flowering time of the honey grevillea, typically November or December

kampuṟarpa (Y)	bush tomato, *Solanum centrale*
kanyaḻa	euro (hill kangaroo), *Macropus robustus*
kata	head
kataṯa	exit holes from animal burrows
kiṯi	adhesive gum made from spinifex resin
kuḻi	hot weather, summer
kuniya	woma python, *Aspidites ramsayi*
kurkara, kukapi	desert oak, *Allocasuarina decaisneana*
kurku	mulga; sweet secretions produced by red lac scale on branches of mulga
langka, lungkaṯa	Centralian blue-tongue lizard, *Tiliqua multifasciata*
latja	edible paste made from ground seeds and water
linga	central netted-dragon, *Ctenophorus nuchalis* military dragon, *Ctenophorus isolepis*
liru (P), *wami* (Y)	mulga snake, *Pseudechis australis* western brown snake, *Pseudonaja nuchalis*
mai wiyaringkupai	a time when food is scarce
maku	edible grubs or caterpillars, esp. witchetty grubs
mala	rufous hare-wallaby, *Lagorchestes hirsutus*
maḻu	red plains kangaroo, *Macropus rufus*
manta aṯunymankupai	looking after country
mangata, wayanu (P)	quandong, *Santalum acuminatum*
maṟutjara	thunder clouds

mingkiri (see *tarkawara, anula, wiltjinypa, murtja)*	small mice and marsupials, including:
	sandy inland mouse, *Pseudomys hermannsburgensis*
	desert mouse, *P. desertor*
	house mouse (introduced), *Mus musculus*
	wongai ningaui, *Ningaui ridei*
	Ooldea dunnart, *Sminthopsis ooldea*
	hairy-footed dunnart, *S. hirtipes*
	lesser hairy-footed dunnart, *S. youngsoni*
mingkulpa, pulyantu	native tobacco (pituri), *Nicotiana excelsior, N. gossei*
miniri, ngiyari	thorny devil, *Moloch horridus*
mirilyirilyi	fairy wrens, *Malurus* spp.
	dusky grasswren, *Amytornis purnelli*
	striated grasswren, *A. striatus*
mitika, tjungku	burrowing bettong, *Bettongia lesueur*
mulutinpa	unidentified lizard
murtja	mulgara, *Dasycercus cristicauda*
mutinka	small skinks, including:, *Ctenotus schomburgkii, C. brooksi, C. dux, C. quattuordecimlineatus, C. leonhardii, C. piankai, C. leae, C. septenarius, Menetia greyii*
muur-muurpa, itara	bloodwood tree, *Eucalyptus opaca*
muya-muya	a grub found on mulga leaves
ngapala	dwarf bearded dragon, *Pogona minor*
ngintaka	perentie, *Varanus giganteus*
ninu (P) *tjalku* (Y)	bilby, *Macrotis lagotis*

nyaṟu	burnt-out country
nyaṟuni	to clear country by burning
nyii-nyii	zebra finch, *Poephila guttata*
nyuma	seed cake or damper
pakuta, palpa	horse mulga, *Acacia ramulosa*
papangaurpa, wauṟa	fat-tailed gecko, *Diplodactylus conspicillatus*
	three-lined knob-tail, *Nephrurus levis*
	smooth knob-tail, *N. laevissimus*
	beaked gecko, *Rhynchoedura ornata*
parka-parka	mistletoe, *Lysiana murrayi*
partjata, kuninka	western quoll, *Dasyurus geoffroii*
paṯiny-paṯinypa	Burton's snake-lizard, *Lialis burtonis*
pila	sandplains
Piṟanpa	non-Aboriginal person or people
piriya-piriya	springtime when warm winds come from the north and west
piṟurpa	spiny-tailed gecko, *Diplodactylus ciliaris*
	Centralian dtella, *Gehyra montium*
puḻi	rocky areas, hills
puḻtanpa	unidentified lizard
puṉṯaṟu, malpuntari	little button-quail, *Turnix velox*
puraṟa	worker ants of the honey ant *(tjaḻa)*
putukalya	dragon lizard, *Tympanocryptis lineata*
tali	sandhills

tarkawara	spinifex hopping-mouse, *Notomys alexis*
tjakura	great desert skink, *Egernia kintorei*
	?nocturnal desert skink, *E. striata*
	?narrow-banded sand-swimmer, *Eremiascincus fasciolatus*
	?small skink, *Ctenotus helenae*
tjala	honey ant, *Camponotus* spp., esp. *C. inflatus*
tjaliri	small to medium skinks, including: *Ctenotus helenae, C. pantherinus, Cyclodomorphus branchialis, Egernia inornata*
tjampuni	an emu chick which travels at a distance from its parents and other chicks
tjanpi kiti	gummy spinifex, *Triodia pungens*
tjanpi	spinifex, *Triodia* spp., esp. *T. irritans*
tjilkamata, tjirilya	echidna, *Tachyglossus aculeatus*
tjintjira	claypan, claypan filled with water
tjiranka	pre-adolescent
Tjukurpa	Anangu Law
tjunguringkula waakaripai	working together
tjuntalpa	clouds coming from the south, associated with cold weather
tjuntalpi	long-nosed dragon, *Lophognathus longirostris*
	canegrass two-lined lizard, *Diporiphora winneckei*
tjuratja	sweet substance, such as nectar and honeydew and sugary scale found on gum leaves
tjuta	many
ulpuru	a habitat favoured by kangaroos

urtjanpa, katji (Y)	spear bush, *Pandorea doratoxylon*
utuwar̲i	overcast weather, but not much rain
wakalpuka (P), kurara (Y)	dead finish, *Acacia tetragonophylla*
walkalpa, tjila (Y)	emu poison bush, *Duboisia hopwoodii*
wanari (P), kurku (Y)	mulga, *Acacia aneura*
wanitjunkupayi	animals hibernating
waputi, pukara	desert thryptomene, *Thryptomene maisonneuvei*
wari	cold time of year
waru	black-footed rock-wallaby, *Petrogale lateralis*
watarka	umbrella bush, *Acacia ligulata*
wayut̲a, mungawayur̲u	brushtail possum, *Trichosurus vulpecula*
wiltjinypa	kultarr, *Antechinomys laniger*
	long-tailed dunnart, *Sminthopsis longicaudata*
	sandhill dunnart, *S. psammophila*
	desert mouse, *Pseudomys desertor*
wintaru, nyul̲u	golden bandicoot (extinct), *Isoodon auratus*
witjinti	corkwood tree, *Hakea suberea*

Pronunciation guide to Pitjantjatjara and Yankunytjatjara

Pitjantjatjara and Yankunytjatjara are two of the many dialects of the Western Desert language which covers an extensive area of Central and Western Australia.

The following pronunciations are a guide only. There are sounds in Pitjantjatjara and Yankunytjatjara which cannot be represented by English spellings because they don't exist in English. Please note:

1. Some English words have been used (e.g. jaw, Paul, come, pay) to show the sound. Otherwise, you can presume the syllable shown will rhyme with a common word, for example the 'nung' sound for An̲angu rhymes with 'sung'.
2. Syllables in bold type are stressed.

Pitjantjatjara	English style pronunciation	Pitjantjatjara	English style pronunciation
ailuru	**ay** loo roo	*apar̲a*	**ah** pah rah
akal̲pa	**ah** call pah	*aral̲apal̲pal̲pa*	**ah** rull ah **paul** paul pah
An̲angu	**ah** nung oo	*arngul̲i*	**ah** noo lee
anula	**ah** nool lah	*arutju*	**a** roo joo

aṯunymankupai	**ah** doon **marn** goo **pay**
ikarka	**ee** kah kah
iḻi	**ear** lee
inma	**in** mah
inuntji	**in** oon jee
iraṯi	**ee** rah dee
iṯaṟa	**ee** tah rah
itjanu	**ee** jah noo
itjaritjari	**eat** jar eat jar ee
kaḻaya	**kah** lah yah
kaliny-kalinypa	**cull** in **cull** in pah
kampuṟarpa	**come** poor rah pah
kanyaḻa	**carn** yah lah
Kata Tjuṯa	**kah** dah **jaw** dah
kataṯa	**kah** dah dah
katji	**kah** jee
kiṯi	**kee** dee
kukapi	**cook** ah pee
kuḻi	**cool**ie
kuninka	**coo** nin gah
kuniya	**coo** nee ah
kupaṯa	**coo** bah dah
kuṟara	**coo** rah rah
kurkaṟa	**core** kah rah
kurku	**cuck**oo
langka	**loong** gah
latja	**lah** jah
linga	**ling** ah
liru	**leer** roo
lungkaṯa	**loong** gah dah
mai	may
maku	**mah** goo
mala	**mah** lah
malpuntari	**mull** boon durry
maḻu	**mah** loo
mangaṯa	**mung** ah dah

manta	**marn** dah
marutjara	**mar** roo jah rah
mingkiri	**ming** gear ee
mingkulpa	**ming** gall pah
miniri	**mi**ni ree
mirilyirilyi	**mee** rill yee rill yee
mitika	**mi**di car
mulutinpa	**more** loo din pah
mungawayuru	**moong** ah way you roo
murtja	**more** jah
mutinka	**more** din gah
Mutitjulu	**moo** dee joo loo
muur-muurpa	**more** more pah
muya-muya	**moo** yah **moo** yah
ngapala	**nah** pah lah
ngintaka	**nin** dah kah
ngiyari	**nee** yah ree
ninu	**nee** noo
nyaru	**nyah** roo
nyaruni	**nyah** roo nee
nyii-nyii	**nyee** nyee
nyulu	**new** loo
nyuma	**new** mah
pakuta	**park** or dah
palpa	**parl** pah
papangaurpa	**pah** pung hour pah
parka-parka	**bark**er **bark**er
partjata	**par** jut ah
patiny-patinypa	**pah** din **pah** din pah
pila	**bill** ah
Piranpa	**peer** un pah
piriya-piriya	**peer** ee yah **peer** ee yah
pirurpa	**peer** roo pah
Pitjantjatjara	**pigeon** jarrer
pukara	**book** ah rah
puli	**bul**ly

pultanpa	**paul** dun bah
pulyantu	**pull** yarn do
puntaru	**porn** da roo
purara	**poor** rah rah
putukalya	**put** do gull yah
tali	**tah** lee
tarkawara	**tuck**er worra
tjakipiri	**jah** key peer ee
tjakura	**jah** core rah
tjala	**jah** lah
tjaliri	**jah** lee ree
tjalku	**jull** coo
tjampuni	**jum** bore nee
tjanpi	**jarn** bee
tjantjalka	**jarn** jull kah
tjila	**jill** ah
tjilkamata	**jill** gah mah dah
tjintjira	**jin** jeer ah
tjiranka	**jeer** run gah
tjirilya	**jeer** rill yah
Tjukurpa	**jook** oor pah
tjungku	**joong** goo
tjunguringkula	**joong** or ring coo lah
tjuntalpa	**jawn** dull pah
tjuntalpi	**jawn** dull pee
tjuratja	**jaw** rah jah
ulpuru	**ool** pour roo
Uluru	**ool** oo roo
urtjanpa	**or** jun pah
utuwari	**oo** do worry
waakaripai	**wah** curry pay
wakalpuka	**wog**gle booker
walkalpa	**woll** gull pah
wami	**wum**my
wanari	**one** ah ree
wanitjunkupai	**one** ee **joon** goo pay

wapuṯi	**wop** or dee
wari	**wor**ry
waru	**worr**oo
waruṟungkalpa	**wor**roo **roong** gull bah
waṯarka	**what** ah kah
wauṟa	**wuh** oora
wayaṉu	**why** yah nah
wayuṯa	**why** your dah
wiltjinypa	**will** jin bah
wintaru	**win** dah roo
witjinti	**witch** indy
wiyaringkupai	**we** ah **ring** goo pay
Yankunytjatjara	**young** goon jarrer

Bibliography

CSIRO, 1993, 'Uluru Fauna: the distribution and abundance of vertebrate fauna of Uluru (Ayers Rock–Mount Olga) National Park, NT,' by J. R. W. Reid, J. A. Kerle & S. R. Morton, *Kowari*, number 4, Australian National Parks and Wildlife Service, Canberra.

Goddard, C. 1987, *A Basic Pitjantjatjara/Yankunytjatjara to English Dictionary*, Institute for Aboriginal Development, Alice Springs.

Goddard, C. 1992, *Pitjantjatjara/Yankunytjatjara to English Dictionary*, 2nd edition, Institute for Aboriginal Development, Alice Springs.

Goddard, C. & Kalotas, A. (eds) 1988, *Punu: Yankunytjatjara plant use*, IAD Press, Alice Springs.

Latz, P. 1995, *Bushfires & Bushtucker: Aboriginal plant use in Central Australia,* IAD Press, Alice Springs.